Not Knowing Itself

Marita Over

ARROWHEAD
PRESS

First published 2006 by
Arrowhead Press
70 Clifton Road, Darlington
Co. Durham, DL1 5DX
Tel: (01325) 260741

Typeset in 11pt Laurentian by
Arrowhead Press

Email: editor@arrowheadpress.co.uk
Website: http://www.arrowheadpress.co.uk

Arrowhead Press acknowledges the financial assistance of
Arts Council England, North East.

Arrowhead Press is a member of
Independent Northern Publishers.

Printed by Athenaeum Press, Gateshead, Tyne and Wear.

for Mum and Dad, with love

Acknowledgements

Thanks are due to the editors of the following publications in which some of the poems in this book have appeared:

Ambit
Chimera
Metre
The Rialto
Smith's Knoll
Stand
The Times Literary Supplement

Thanks also to the following for all their help and support:
Malcolm Burgess, Julia Casterton, Tim Cunningham, Isobel Lusted, Jeremy Over, Heather Reyes and the Cumbrian Poets

Cover Picture – *Woman by a River* – watercolour
© *Marita Over 2006*

Contents

Supposing

The fire has really slumped.
A while ago when a gust of air
snuck under the door, it glowed.
But since then it's been slipping away.

We've half a mind to save it:
if we built a wigwam of kindling over it,
poked a few holes through its delicate ash
and stretched a few leaves of broadsheet across,

it could be seized with a hankering to live –
a new appetite, like waking at 5 am
with nothing on your mind
but bacon and eggs.

A sudden orangeness could illuminate
the inside of the printed sheets
like a pair of insect's wings
being pumped into life.

But if we weren't careful to pull the sheets away in time,
the inner pages might catch
and we'd have this roaring fireball in our outstretched arms
like an awful baby we couldn't do anything to stop,

and we'd be forced to let it go then
flying up the chimney,
and we'd have to listen out
in case it set the roof on fire.

And after a time, after a time,
all the sooty little pieces would come
floating and spinning down
to blacken the neighbour's lawn.

Tuesday

I'd start in my front garden
on the splashy red cherry leaves
on a wet November morning.
Then I'd go on
and sweep the playground
when the kids weren't there
and the alley
where the little white dog
yaps and craps behind its fence
and on to the rough pub car park,
just pushing along the broken glass
and the empty boxes of Marlboro.
I'd sweep those boring motorways
up to my mother's county,
the burnt out, abandoned scrap
and the loops of rubber tyre,
the puddles in the Midland's shopping malls.
Up and down the parks
of Northern England I would go
down avenues of chestnut
sweeping their fallen star shapes
with that lovely effort
of stretching and pulling
pushing and hoarding
coaxing along the bilge on rivers, estuaries, canals.
And I'd work my way back down again
trailing the wet west coast
then in, but short of the suburbs,
along the country lanes of the comfortable South
curling the dust like a butter pat
rolling it over and over itself
till it formed a fat sort of cylinder.
And I'd roll it down to the English Channel
that poor weary housewife collapsing – repeatedly –
at Swanage.
From there I'd bear east-south-east

across the Straits of Dover
till I came in the evening
to sad Dunkirk.
And I'd sweep those beaches
gently as a tongue
probing for tiny cavities,
or the quavery light of a hand-held torch
searching for missing bodies.
And I'd sweep the whole
of Northern Europe
as wide as my arms could manage,
as if my broom
were a tipped up bottle
of lively wine
that washed as it stained these far flung lands
of my goutish, large-toothed forefathers.
Fjords and forests
the grey Dutch dunes,
cloudberries nestled in shaggy moss
round the clustered lakes of Finland.
And into the cupboards of petty strife,
I'd foist the nose of my ordinary broom,
into municipalities, histories,
into the industries,
into the bourgeois love of husband and wife
the blues of desolate adolescence
the raw, yellow waking
of angry babies all over Europe, wailing.
And then someday
I'd take my broom
back to the land of my childhood,
to the central plateau
of the vast Ethiopian highlands,
land of the mountain nyala
and the olive-coloured baboon.

I'd go to those rocks
where man first fell
for want of a rope or tail.
And there, on the peak of Mount Ras Deshen
jewel of the Simien mountains
I'd raise my broom to the clouds I knew
when I was small
and had no besom
but watched an old woman up in a basket
seventeen times as high as the moon.
And with my final, biggest effort
I'd sweep those cumulonimbus
out of the sky.
And you might be there
noticing
wanting to know if by and by
all would be well again
and I would please come home
and tuck us up in bed again.
But you'd never guess how far I'd been
And no-one , not even you,
would really notice the difference –
as any housewife will tell you
who's been hard at it all morning
sweeping the dreams off the lawn.

Hot Air

A vapour trail slowly strikes
a three-legged camel
then a shoe manifests itself
up in the sky.

Over the hedge comes
half a conversation.
The headmaster's wife
as she chops at the laurel.

Her voice is like a warm cake
pressed in its tin,
a certain humour bubbling the crumb,
the odd glacé cherry

which drops to the grass now
where a handful of ants
have organised themselves
a brassband and a cream tea – also

a raffle and a day trip to the seaside
that will never come off:
they are all too stingy
to put money in the kitty.

Just carry on heaving out their
leatherette suitcases
and rummaging tinily – the noise of sugar –
for socks and pants and roadmaps.

The long afternoon fills
its silky empty self
up to its knot until
there is no such thing at all.

Stroking the Seconds

It's close in the room, but sappy
with plane trees practically
sprawling in through the open window,
while Lytton's mother-of-pearl shirt buttons
are definitively fastened to his throat.

A platoon of street heat
breaks gently into the room
and rifles through the papers on our desk.
"Why," it whispers, "this is nothing," then badmouths
me in my crumpled shift on the stained chaise longue, for indolence.

And lastly, nonchalantly,
lifts this leaf of sun-singed, papery skin
which is mine, I own, and yet no-one's –
just a sort of thumbprint
stitched at my raw shoulder;

or perhaps a microfiched piece of scandal
– a newspread the size of a postage stamp
for emmets to dribble and pore over.
But think of the way you can even dawdle
over stamps ...

From two until four,
I watch it rise and fall
like a ragged moth practising
some out of fashion steps
for a ball it isn't going to.

From four until five, I ease it off, painfully
counting its perforations. Then,
at ten past five, Lytton runs his long-
tipped index finger
down another index:

every consonant catches his beautiful nail –
like a washboard's frictive beading.
All that evenness of print just too like
a deathly wallpaper a bluebottle must
drag its scaly wings across.

"At least murmur the word you're looking for, can't you?"
"If you're ever stuck in a lift with a stranger,
wait a full hour, at least, before you commence
exchanging glances," he suggests.

The seventh delivery van in the street this month
deranges the china cabinet gracelessly.
Then Strachey's great head moves a fraction –
he lifts his chin, I imagine,
to sense the light-beneath-water air brush past his lips

which he just pressed together, so interestingly,
tasting the 'm' in 'motionless'.

Letter to Jacek Podsiadlo
(after Letter From the Land of the Red Roofs. To Anna-Maria)

i

I'm making coffee for the air again. A bright green lacewing
is thinking on my typewriter.
Open the window onto the morning's square.
Already traffic and a queue from Ulica Putawska to Ulica Piekna
for the latest Podsiadlo collection. We wish.
Love, here is the morning's broadsheet
opening like a pigeon stretching a giant accordion over the roofs,
and everyone knows it will
all fold in again, the share index collapse
and this coffee go sulky like ink in its pot
because you're not here to drink it with me.
Lacewings have no sense of smell.
You say you've been listening to cows in their wistful mooing:
better you go and milk one, Jacek.
Or better still, go pick more of those wild raspberries in your woods.
We all go a little wild and moony alone too long.
And the lack of proper shelter would make things worse....

God help us, Jacek, I woke up not knowing where I was.
You weren't beside me, and neither was *he.*
I had an hour to drowse and to slip in and out
of the wings of a childhood puppet theatre
where it seems I had lost a handkerchief –
or was it one of my children?
It was dark. The king, queen and jester
were all in a heap, asleep, their strings in terrible knots.

Losing a piece of yourself is good every once in a while.
But the dread is that someone will find you,
and deliver you back to yourself, in person, by hand.

Please understand that I have whole cities
in these padlocked cupboards
that, sadly, I can never share with you.

Love, when you know what to do, come back.
Meanwhile, light your candle for me.

ii

As usual, you had no idea
where you were. Pity.
I might have found a way
to send you my reply.

What will become of us?
Whatever does,
there's only me to bear the cross.
Your coming back to share it would be useless.

And you jumped on that train this time
leaving us nothing – no coin
to put in the meter or tin.
So what do I say to *him*?

You woke in the rain you say
in a book in the sky
or some such crazy thing – why
tell me these things – to make me cry?

Candles burnt, smokes all gone.
Unclean bed, this woman worn
down to a stump and a frown
that you wouldn't stuff in a sack with a cat to drown.

Spiders

A Rorschach inkblot is
fastened on the porcelain.
Will not respond at first, nor wash away.
Does not thin. Does not appear

to bloom into a colour chart
like those ink chromatograms
whose wet throats bleed the secrets of their
blackest composition.

It is an alert black hand
around my heart, squeezing it dry.
This is a stain that stays.
No lady can easily wash it away.

Yet all through October
the creature thrived on our lavender.
Females fattened
gently in their spinnings.

Soft flesh, speckled
like mute thrushes,
or sun-warmed miniature toads
intent on digestion.

And our garden all autumn
like a good sleep you wake from
the threads to your hinterland cut and forgotten,
contained them out of sight and mind.

November now though, with both taps on,
the gushing lifts her too light body
on a swirl that spins her
drifting towards the plug-hole.

There she staggers, little hag,
on a penny-pinching stint,
making thrifty
silk of the water.

Rape Fields at Ingatestone
(After Emil Nolde)

Deep in the reed beds
a pond skater tests the surface tension.

Under a strong, fruit-syrupy light,
a field of rape begins to tremble.
Evening is falling like a net
of escaping minutiae
hauled up
and yet falling,
slippery from a sky that mingles
crimsonness with bewilderment.

Two fields away
three anxious oaks'
synapses crackle with static.
Waist-deep in the yellow-crop,
they transmit one last queasy thought: go.
And though in doubt,
a youngish copse
has taken heed and begun to drift
slowly down its distant hill.

It will leave behind
this chaos of colour,
to go slipping over
the glassy rim of the mind
that can hold
no lasting mark
of its ever having been here.

The careful pond skater
settles his wings
as I climb down stalks
to his magnified creases,
then lie gazing up, my back
to his back,
feeling his ridges, stilled.

And I steer my childhood gondola
through all the papery irises,
watching their stems above me
turning dark.

Desire

Carries itself like a tipsily-held glass
of the darkest-staining claret.
Has no idea of decorum,
leans violently out
on high-rise ledges on rainy nights
in gowns that cling with the static of cobwebs.

Crackles and buzzes like faulty wiring
and at any moment might
break out in flames.
Runs like a ladder
on the shoulder of a fool
into the core of chaos it creates.

It is our house on fire –
yes, our house on fire
whose windows
ball the curtains in a sudden fist.

It jerks a fevered wrist
shovelling tender nothings
into its furnace.
And all the while
its parted lips,
try to recite the one about the boy –
that obstinate, stammering
transparent boy –
and the flames
the ineluctable flames
which took him
crackling
down.

Coming Back

We told no-one what we saw that day –
the child like a hornet's nest
hanging in the stairwell.

We promised each other we wouldn't.

I'm depending solely on
remnants of memory
to find my way back.

Under the spell of stillness so long,
it won't open itself to me.

My shoes stir the dust
as I cross each room.

I remember how we'd first spread out,
each of us cocooned
in our own curiosity.

I joggle a drawer agape on its tired runners.
It opens up an emptiness.
A newspaper's print on a slatted base,
transferred back-to-front,
might give some dates

if I had the right mind to read them.

Wardrobe mirrors tremble on sudden discovery.
Things lack ornament.

A mug hangs in artless suspense
from a hook on a dirty dresser.

In the iron grate
we built some splintered sticks
like fingers crossed for prayer,
but we had no matches to light them.

He touched my breasts then under my vest,
I pressed him down in that armchair
and made him wait.

We both knew who had made the boy do it.

One of the others fetched a pan
of water from the scullery
and we rubbed with a rag at the stains
but the water just wasn't warm enough.

You can't account for time.
Cold light falling through an upstairs window
is suddenly afternoon.

And we came downstairs that evening
in ones and twos
hemmed in by the need for an adult.

We rattled the big door open again
and picked our way back through the woods
where a thinnish rain jumped at our skin
and niggled us back into life.
The youngest found a hefty stick
and strode on in front: we let him.

Rain falls now
as I walk through the woods back home.
Its touch releases the scent
of spring-coiled ferns
like a mother
who in turning her child's pillow
to blank bad dreams,
somehow releases her own.

Journey

You were walking across my body,
making a small scuffed path
in the light snow.

A westerly wind was picking up
over the ridge of my pelvic bone.
You were dogged in your trail

head down, unaware that your weight
prickled my skin as your tread
came up towards my diaphragm.

I tightened the whole of my abdomen,
straining my head and shoulders up,
even wrongly lifted my hips

trying to tilt you back into the dip of my belly,
but it was too late to stop you : you'd crossed
the rock of my sternum and your knees

were bending and straightening,
pushing through the heavier drifts
that had gathered in the shallow between my breasts.

I sank back down.
Clouds lowered slantwise
and let a gentle aching of rain sweep through the middle ground.

Then it seemed you'd gone.
I stared at the footprints you had made
at the beginning of your journey,

pressed my finger into one
as if I were laying a coin
on a recently warm eyelid.

The Tenants

Two sly red snakes
are alive in the cupboard
where the water pipes are warm.
Because there are two
it is difficult
to keep track of them
and above all else
we must do that: know
which gaping door
or lumpy blanket
they might slip out from.

How do they get here?

Perhaps we accidentally
bring them into the house
as eggs or thoughts
on our clothes or hair –
in our looks.

The slack track of them
side-loops across the carpets
seeking out comfort.
Their length and girth is astonishing;
their colour – raw steak.
They carry their heads like kings
as if they bore glass candelabra aloft
to light the dark.

We must remember they are blind and depend on heat.
I'll keep the house cold.
Perhaps they will leave of their own accord.

Haircut

This time the amount shocks the lino'd floor.

When you run upstairs to the bathroom
I kneel down to look at it.

With both hands slightly damp,
I lift the black curled animal.

Here is
a road accident.
Here is
the floppy
sack of someone's
strength.

It is an afterbirth,
a muscled will, felled.

I must bury
the long, shining loop of it,
deep in the rubbish,
wrap it up in paper
so none of it escapes.

Upstairs I can hear you
running from room to room
checking in all the mirrors.

There's a sense in the house
as if the tongue of a bell
had been – not removed but – clamped to one side.
I go about my business
nervous and resolute
as if the midwife had watched me
cut the cord myself.

Sunday Afternoons

In the nursery's warm plastic wind tunnel,
the air is moist and eases breathing.

Light has stewed to the greeny-gold
of gunpowder tea in a jam jar.

Tomatoes drag themselves up ropes,
bound to the ridgepoles of the tunnel's arc.

The moment you touch them, they split,
and a hot yellow sprawl tingles to be licked better like a graze.

The afternoon so still,
you can hear the fuchsia droop

and racks of pelargonium sigh, stretch
and overlap their leggy growth

like the synchronised swimming Busby Babes
in their matching floral bathing caps.

If no-one were here but you,
you might clamber onto the pocket-sprung

mattresses of bedding plants
to take a quiet siesta,

your ear pressed to the jostling
of the squeaky, mewling new-borns

in their polystyrene boxes,
starting to root for their nourishment.

The Clarity

Sunlight lit on the down of her arms.
I felt sick knowing what I was going to do.

I was at the Sorbonne that summer.

My Dutch friend – I'd known her three months –
had come to Paris to sign up for studies.
I don't remember her subject.
She sat on the edge of my sofa
lifting the thimble of coffee
to her thick-cut, dark red lips.
But I was not interested in her sex.
I was already feeling weak
as if water, not blood,
dribbled through me.

She looked so bright.

I felt the moment invisibly pinned
like a damselfly midflight.

She wasn't the type I like to seduce.
Her face was not oriental.
Her nose – I don't know – was perhaps too long.
Her bosom bumped and swayed too heavy
as she leaned to put her cup
on the glass-topped table.

I don't recall our conversation.
I think it was mostly general.

The air in the room was convalescent.

I remember thinking so many things:
where I might be ten years from that day
should I live that long.
I remembered the drooping wisteria pods
on my mother's silvered pergola
and the painted screen on which she would hang
my towel and undergarments.
She would send me down each afternoon
to splash feebly in the pool
always standing too far back,
her attention attaching itself to the koi
or to this or that reflection. A cloud, a stick,
a leaf but never my limbs.
I became transparent before her.

My Dutch friend rose
to inspect the Mondrian over the bureau
and in doing so pressed on the french-polished walnut
a sweat spot that instantly lifted.
I was grateful for that reminder
to notice what else she might touch.

The rest of the week was full
of many such practical considerations.

As usual the contemplation of the act
surpassed in terms of pleasure the act itself.

I did not like draining her.

All I had to sustain me
through those hours of preparation
was imagining the light in her skin
filling me up like milk.

I will not go into those details here in this interview.

Yes, I was released.

Yes, I am currently making a film.
I have a celebrity's status.

My mother.

Electronic tagging
to keep them alert to my whereabouts.

No, I am never safe.

The moment I felt I'd reached safety
was by the fourth or fifth cut from her calf.

Field and Hook

The tears in his eyes
were so real. So real
we looked at him and felt
our own welling up.

It could've meant anything.
It could've been anyone.

Please forgive me all
forgive me.

*

A field and the hook
so intimate with each other
that I couldn't bear it.

Field running all the way
as if it had legs
down towards the crease in itself
and we were just following, striving
carefully across
as if we were stuck down on flypaper,
its ruffled burnt sienna
collecting in drifts
as it ran with a quickness
we couldn't outstrip.

Then spring yielding
out of it a gentle fluff
so that we talked about razing, razoring

doing unto

always
doing unto
oh let a first law be
to let be all things. Stop
the neurotic twitching to meaning,
to adjustment of meaning: let that field be
as it is, was, as now and ever shall – but hook –
we forgot: look.

It comes out of the oakwoods
curved, glinting; could destroy
the whole,
from these nothing
micro-organisms that I
imagine dwelling on the surface of my eye
right to where my heart spills over the edge.
Splinter of mirror
in the eye of a boy
blinded and dragged
to the cruellest extreme of eternal winter.
Field and hook intimate   as breath.

But from that very edge comes
summer: its quavering singing Let
fleecy flocks the hills adorn and smile
with wavy corn. Let fleecy flocks
the hills adorn, the hills adorn …
and smile with wavy corn.

Which of you would stand in it,
say to the waist, holding up a restraining hand –
the tears in your eyes, when it comes to it?
None, I say, none, none. Not
all the glory rising in the frothy lace of circling gulls,
in our moments of crescendo, the corn swaying, waving,
could ever bring a single

god up through the eyelet.
Oh bring it down. Let
brown November
isolate each symptom
so that field becomes
a catalogue
a dull, remorseless matte
pinched of lifesap,
of opulence,
its oily Giorgione greens,
the chinese blue of oak leaves so
never-before-noticed of high summer.
It happens. It was happening there and then,
until I turned around and I said,
"Not worth hanging onto,
not worth the millions of creative explosions,
implosions – all the activity,
the great mess of protoplasm – even the idea of it
tiring –
just not worth hanging onto, lover boy."
"Even nature can't let be," someone thought somewhere.
"To be divine is to act upon,
to push
each
thing
to its outer boundaries..."
"And there abandon it, " I thought.

And at that point I really wanted to put the thing away,
even with a sealed December sky genuflecting
into the shadows of the hillocky rucks and blessing them
with an indigo deep as coal's flames. Even then, then, then,
the wish
rising in me,
which was more like a sinking when I come to think of it...

*

She said, "That was sad."
She said, "If nothing else,
        it *was* sad."
And she closed the book
but her thumb was still in the page,
and I could see in her lowered left eye
a red fleck
bursting its single cell capillary boundaries –
un-
stemmable
tiny
corneal
haemorrhage
spilling over onto the sheets,
come like a shadow over the wheat,
or to put it in the negative,

like the shocking bones
out of the ploughed ground.

Lines after Wang Wei
i.m. Pete

Slash of blue rain
across the windows of a train
that passes by your station
more than twenty times a day

and you no longer there,
but bones on a hill
too far away from here
and my ticket taking me further.

*

And your hands
blue and bitten, stained and gentle
that loved to hold the wings of books
so close to you as if they might fly off

now just bird-sticks
under the earth
and your silence now, as often on the phone,
so hard to listen to.

Pulling over in a lay-by in Green's Farm Lane

to gaze on
the dreaming fox
that lies beside the verge
head pushed back, mouth open,
his sandy cheek
pressed to its cold pillow.

The rain has stopped
and like a slow-warming oil,
the sky becomes striated in the east
over the crowded roof-tops of the housing estate.

The radio voices turn intrusive –
I switch it off.

In the back in the dark sits my son, quiet,
fingers curled on a plastic horse,
his features in the rear-view mirror
still and bright.

And in the lane, the gorse has begun to free
some colour through its thorny spines.

Love spills on,
not careless exactly
but approximate,
not quite brutal.

Difficult Poem

At the end of the path
the hawthorn arches
over a view of fields.
The one view.

Clouds well up like chores
and a great sadness
over in the east,
above the woods.

Sometimes I like that.

If nothing suggests itself soon
I won't be able
to look much longer;

fabrication bears down
like a strange-smelling hand
to cover my face.

Nonsense
for Finn born 29/02/96

Take these records to your private den, Finn: you'll
open them in your own time, like gifts.
At three and a half you named nearly fifty
flowers; at four, you spouted Lewis Carroll
– backwards when you'd half a mind for it.
At five, these spurious-sounding insects would alight
from the tip of your tongue, compelling us
to check them with your sources – you'd be right.
We didn't push. That Leap Day, we just
breathed as you were sucked into the light.
And it seemed even then that a magical force
in the glass ventouse chamber let you loose.
Genius. Fairy's child, with no real sense
ever to know how *we'd* feel, your difference.

Testing the Salt

Bad dreams propel me out of bed at 5 am,
down to the frozen dark to scalp the lawn;
to chop the turf clean off the stubborn clay
hard-wired with bright worms that bulge chubbily
then ease themselves out like crocodile tears
squeezed from the kind of kids Finn isn't: the kind
who loll their tongues to test the salt: who hear
and adjust their sobs to best effect and find
all they need to know, with all their means. Finn
these days just tilts his head back, juts his chin
and tries to stop tears running down his cheeks because
the touch is more than he can manage. Work draws
warmth to the fingertips, but nothing will thaw
clay while the winter sun's so low.

Magnetic Resonance Imaging

The difference between us here is that I
believe in scientific investigation.
I like its painstaking methods and limited 'I';
its commitment to control and exact replication:
practical skill, the warp to hypothetical weft.
You dismiss it because it can't explain
consciousness or delve into meaning – but what's left
undiscussed is how we feel about Finn's scan.
You'd say that throwing nerves in patterns on a screen
is not the way to deal with our pain – why, when
we already have such intimate knowledge
push further in and gaze at the damage?
Yet seeing the matter lit in grey relief
might illuminate the boundaries to our grief.

Soap

Back from a weekend with your dad, and for
a day or so, again, you seem reluctant
to let me help unpack your bags or settle
into your space here. Won't reclaim the chair
you sit sideways in to negotiate soaps
over the white water rapids of Finn's steady roar
as he runs to and fro across the rucked and
choppy carpet. The TV and the kettle
stay cold. Gentle and polite you keep a hair's
breadth back from us while, unseen, X elopes
with Y; Y's father threatens to kill X but
X's mother was once his lover, so
X could be his son ... ours is not that kind of plot
but one you still have to slip back through glass into.

Refrigerator Parents

"Once you've met a few you'll easily
spot their parents too", one aficionado
tips me over hors d'oeuvres. Queasily
I withdraw to the nearest loo.
One ballroom and a corridor between us
I rinse and dry my hands to stop them shaking;
pin on my tag to stop anyone else
mistaking me for a therapist. Then faking
a look of ironic amusement I thrust
my tics into an inscrutable darkness
like scraps of evidence no-one must
ever find – bits of a still-warm carcass.
Imperative to freeze in a cold store
things that would bleed if they began to thaw.

Swans

We've slipped the children off like bracelets
and come down to the tow path at Baddow
to walk freely, swing our arms and talk about
everything. I show you in the shadow
of a certain poplar, wild irises as tall as man
disguising themselves as flecks of light.
You liken a cormorant on the other bank to an
old junked umbrella stumbling into flight
and we'd go further, beyond the lock, but it's then
that we see the odd-looking trio. They might
be you and me and Finn thirty years on.
The middle-aged son hurls bread to some cygnets
under the arch gaze of swans who privately know
that the purpose of rearing young is to let them go.

Tree Frogs

"If one met a truthful man and one who
lied walking in opposite directions from
heaven and from hell, how could one tell who
came from where? What question should we ask them?"
Kaspar starts to circle in his hausschuhe
watched by an ageing patron. Herzog's
uncluttered lens documents a steady
ebb of light, like a slow withdrawal of confidence.
A fly dies. The visiting philosopher
doodles boxes in the dark. "Tree frogs!
Ask if they are tree frogs!" beams Kaspar, ready
to dance a jig. Well, genius or dunce,
those tree frogs solve the problem twice:
a truthful mind's reflected in a face.

Documentary

The girl with Asperger's sits on the back step
of her warden-controlled, shared house, a novel
she's just started open on her lap.
Half-smiling at, not quite focused on, the gravel,
she's telling someone why she likes her home.
The morning sun illuminates her face
but can't quite touch the softness which has grown
in her like those new fingertips of asparagus
you don't like to cut. She says it's 'cosy'
as if the word were a beautiful stone
she'd chosen. And I imagine Lucy
eating toast with Tumnus in his den.
The too soft girl I had to shut in a book
in case anyone cruel came up to have a look.

Reading Other Minds

I've imagined what it's like to be you,
Finn, boy who fell out of the sky and found
himself surrounded by swarms of insects
bristling with black purpose, backs towards you,
or faces; so hard to tell which way round
our fronts were. Chinese or Arabic texts,
we wouldn't stay still long enough to be
focused on, let alone translated. Be me
though now, Finn, unable to rest in my own
skin: the sigh of a passer-by and I'm thrown
into instant empathy. Like a train
jogged onto tracks running east when its aim
was south. Life hasn't gone quite the way I planned.
Sometimes it's a handicap to understand.

The Dark Rule

We work while a child mumbles in his sleep.
In a half-dark field, the devil and I,
intimately bound by the slow,
tricky matter of pattern. We reap
a kind of understanding but no joy
as we fasten one foot to another, row
by row. No rules but this: only while he dreams,
curled like a dormouse in his fattened corn,
can we bend ears, bind sheaves, place stooks to gleam
obscurely in the moonlight. By dawn we're gone.
Before the sun comes up to point the hurt;
distinguish the chaff on our hands from their ingrained dirt.
Climbing the stile, I catch my tattered sleeve
and glimpse my child's face tangled in the weave.

The Interrogator

Grief arrived like freezing fog and pitched
his greyness on the lawn. Some days, gloved
up and masked, he strode into our home
to test his anaesthetic on our tongues.
Making notes, he'd throw us random questions which
our mouths would try to answer. He loved
the way we struggled. But I was overcome
by one relentless question that just hung
over everything I thought and did: how live
believing love was mechanistic;
that certain neural deficits kept love
at one remove? I'd stare into that fog so long
that 'how' would change sometimes to 'why' like breath
on glass lifting an ice pattern I'd grown sick of.

Echolalia

We don't tell each other very often
though it was once such an easy thing:
three words. But like homeopathic drops
increased dilution can't weaken
the effects – it magnifies them, making
each renewed succussion more intense; stops
us bandying 'love' around like sugar pills.
Or perhaps Finn's helpless echolalia
did it for us. Our boomeranged 'I love you' s
came home exactly as they left – quick thrills,
easy game. Yet the longer delayed they were
the more really meant. Now his 'I love you' s
can come quietly unbidden – or at least
delays stretch out so they sound free at last.

The Field

I dreamed I was a place between hedgerows,
a small, ploughed field and you had come on tip-toe
as, on a Sunday morning to our bed, to propose
your latest version of a tale: clods, clouds and crows,
you skipped and stumbled up and down the furrows
rhyming this with that, replacing phrase with phrase
the way you do: exact, with shining eyes.
Then stopping, satisfied, you looked around for praise
but I was sealed in the soil underground,
and could not smile or sigh or ruffle up your hair
so that you'd know that I was really still around
just unable to touch you – break through to the air.
And so it is when I'm locked in my head,
cut off from your here and now, as though dead.

Obsessions

Well, I hurtle along with my changing
"dilettantish interests" – spindly dead ends;
a hundred spokes that have no influence
on where the wheel rolls but, by arranging
themselves at intervals, like kindly friends,
enable it to move; take it in turns
to bear my weight. Other times I lean
too hard one way. A mania that takes
my wheel and runs so fast the rubber burns;
friendships get rattled by my love's keen
course of which I've no control, no brakes.
And when we meet a wall I must re-learn
the will's not free: just a bicycle I've found
slowly ticking over with its wheels upturned.

The River

Night. People swarm the banks of the Thames
or maybe, the Seine. In the jumble I'm
alert to a sense that somebody's drowning,
but no-one else seems aware. Across the water
tumbles the pulse of a steel band's rhythms.
The crowd, like flotsam, bob and swing in time.
It could be Day of the Dead or the crowning
or sacking of a monarch. Their laughter,
jangly somehow joyless reels from the torchlit rows
of faces. So I climb above it, arms wide, balancing
on a gleaming parapet, knowing I must dive
into the slink where now a golden fish throws
itself in painful arcs as if it were dancing.
Then I'm in, fully-clothed – and god are we alive!

Letter

Sometimes in my yard
I see a wall of cobwebs
catching whatever blows by:

leaves, insects, seedheads, wisps
of fur, whatever happens to be
flying our way.

My eyes also catch things;
bits of grit, blue smoke,
a red-edged daisy in a patch of neighbour's lawn.

I no longer hide the fact I smoke.
Just sit out in the backyard, draining the Shiraz,
studying little corpses.

I won't trim the curry plant.
I tip an empty watering can;
scratch a patch of birdshit from the bench with the backdoor key.

A beetle in the tin tub
struggles up the smooth side
4 inches, then falls down.

Starts again – 4 inches,
falls back down.
Tries another tack: skirting the diagonal.

4 inches, falls back down.
I could so easily change its life
by lifting it out.

I won't wash up the supper dishes
unless everyone goes to bed.
I'm looking for trouble.

Wake up most mornings
with crumbs in the sheets
and chocolate on the pillow.

Dear You, not getting better.
In spite of the drugs.
In spite of the beautiful weather.

Wasdale

Wool in the hedges like someone's mistakes;
a handkerchief's knots ignored.
I pick out a clump to tease out its fibres,
spin ropes to wind round my wrist.

This small churchground is a throw of jacks
with names and dates of climbers who fell.
But forgetfulness in this careful mist
comes seeping down the mountainside.

Our path takes us higher to a place between the hills
more narrow and yellowing,
fenced delicately from the lower,
cropped squares of pastureland.

Here, thin grasses sigh.
A coarse moss springs back up after each footfall.
Nothing here can have changed
for a thousand years.

Six months ago,
I wrapped my fingers round your damp, puffy wrist
and felt its unsustainable flux
threading its way on out towards its end,
the static bed.

This low pressure brings the insects
down to ground level. There's no easy way
out of the hills. We must turn back on ourselves
and repeat the same steps that brought us here.

In the shadow of the open door

our cat has made a shrew accessible.

A housefly mills about
the broken scruff of its neck, unable to settle.
It flies off a distance
to take another look,
then jaggers back to lick and spit and peek.

But also there at the open throat is a wasp
practically doubled over, its head
buried in the wet.
Its stiff wings are vertical,
back legs clambering minutely,
smoothing and combing the pile of the fur,
pushing back the mouth of the gash
and straddling for better access.
It is intent, rhythmical, zeroed in
as if it had found the meaning of its existence
right here on my cracked up patio.

More flies appear, and now, as if it had woken
from a sleep, the yellow head comes up
and slowly looks about itself
like a puzzled baby stirring from the breast.

Sleep of Seeds

Whose meadow did I sleep in
and slept and slept the sleep of seeds
blown anyplace and left,
no bird noticing?

And what criss-cross patterns,
my face pressed into them,
taking their impression,
smelled so sweet?

And how in sleep
as I turned by a half-turn,
did that criss-cross grass
become the rigging of a ship?

And how did my soul feel so suddenly lost
in a mazy green mechanics
not knowing which way to steer and stay buoyant,
nor how to trust the sleep that carried it faraway?

Quietness and Rain

It's a quiet morning.
House empty.
The doors all ajar
to let more quietness come.

And here are these creamy peonies
exuding a sense of concentration.
Thick scent and wrapped up
light inside the petals mingle
so that you can't tell
one thing from another;
light from fragrance;
the quietness from its morning.

And rain is creeping over everything.
Outdoors, greenery droops;
half-heartedly turns
against the rain's persistence.
It sometimes slides in streaks
straight down the glazing;
stock-still drops that hold your face in them
will quiver, and then slip.
Again, you can't tell one thing from another,
your willing them to fall from your
knowing that they'll fall.

But now through the rain
comes change; a shift of sound;
a rustling sheet,
a negotiation of folds and seams.
Both a flattening and a probing,
like someone else's gloves tried on.
This could be a way through –
snagged threads, a tear in the cloth,
your fingertips touching the rain's.

Arranging Lunch

I'm preparing an extraordinary salad,
lifting and mixing apple chunks
with shorn hair in a wooden bowl.
The hair has a healthful texture.
I haven't yet thought of how it might
suffocate us when we eat it.

Here by the patio a head
has been set upon
a plinth at waist height
which makes it easy to pour
French dressing into the scalp.

I had intended to use a jug
but sense that to reach to the roots
I must delve with my fingers.

And now I have a good knife to hand.
So sharp that pulling it down
the cheek is like the thing they do
to a violin
to obtain a note
an octave higher; the bow
not in contact almost
with the string.

And yes, I see it is my own soft ochre cheek
as it flops away in a swoon
to the plate my head is secured upon.

My own eyes there in my face
are open and smiling, vaguely dreamy,
as if I had sunbathed
and drenched up the whole of a summer.
Now I can see into what was there,
under my freckled skin all these years –
how like pomegranate pips the red cells are.
And that is me and my cheek and my gaze
so stirringly unfocused and relaxed.
And I would love to call you over across the lawn
to come and look,
but don't because by calling
I'd frighten the gaze away and also because
I want this moment of my own strange loving
to last a little longer.

Shorelines

And the sky
not knowing itself
buckles emptily over
its own white breast,
drinking forgetfulness,
face-down like the back of a hand.

And the sea also not knowing itself
washes itself as if it were
washing another's body.
Lovelessly
but intently
it spreads out its paraphernalia
then hesitates to touch
what might be itself after all.
Along the stiffening line of it
runs a whitish lace
wrizzled in the detritus.

And there am I,
so far away,
coming aimlessly into view.